BUT FOR NOW

THE HUGH MACLENNAN POETRY SERIES

Editors: Allan Hepburn and Tracy Ware

TITLES IN THE SERIES

But for Now

Gordon Johnston

McGill-Queen's University Press
Montreal & Kingston • London • Ithaca

ISBN 978-0-7735-4290-7 (paper)
ISBN 978-0-7735-9007-6 (ePDF)
ISBN 978-0-7735-9008-3 (ePUB)

Legal deposit third quarter 2013
Bibliothèque nationale du Québec

Printed in Canada on acid-free paper that is 100% ancient forest
free (100% post-consumer recycled), processed chlorine free

McGill-Queen's University Press acknowledges the support
of the Canada Council for the Arts for our publishing
program. We also acknowledge the financial support of the
Government of Canada through the Canada Book Fund
for our publishing activities.

Library and Archives Canada Cataloguing in Publication

Johnston, Gordon, 1947–, author
But for now / Gordon Johnston.

(Hugh MacLennan poetry series)
Poems.
Issued in print and electronic formats.
ISBN 978-0-7735-4290-7 (pbk.).– ISBN 978-0-7735-9007-6 (ePDF).–
ISBN 978-0-7735-9008-3 (ePUB)

I. Title. II. Series: Hugh MacLennan poetry series

PS8569.O38B88 2013   C811'.54   C2013-903220-7
                                      C2013-903221-5

This book was typeset by Interscript in 9.5/13 New Baskerville.

CONTENTS

BUT FOR NOW

UNTIL THEN

there lay between them, separating them, that same terrible line
of the unknown

Tolstoy, War and Peace

Drift or stumble, we might,
into another catchment.
But for now.

No machine, apparently.
In a minute you'll stop
letting it ring.

How close is Gaddafi
to knowing for certain
the jig is up.

On the height of land
it's almost mid-day, E.S.T.
just steps away.

DREAM GRAVITY

1

Closeup of a young man
   seated on an airplane,
      a week-old beard trimmed
         along his strong jaw.
He could be an actor,
   but the film of sweat on his lip
      and his forehead
         makes me think he's real.
The plane, a mid-sized commercial jet,
   has suffered a severe mechanical failure in flight
      and is coming down towards a crash landing
         over the jungle of Cambodia or Laos.
Cut to a lively airport bar
   somewhere in North America
      where he is telling his friends how, suddenly,
         either by accident or by design,
a landing field appeared in the jungle,
   and they descended towards it.
      He is thinking, but does not say so aloud,
         about events which are both random
and intensely dramatic.

2

A large solid china cabinet
   with many doors and drawers;
      some of the doors have coloured glass panels
         lozenge-shaped
which light up when you sing
   to show the treasures inside,
      the particular glass panel which lights up
         depends on what it is you sing.

3

A Tallis motet plays on my silver iPod,
   which has the surprising ability
      to distil the music into a clear
         almost colourless liquid,
I push the button on the side
   and the liquid drips into a small glass mason jar,
      at first an acid, fiercely strong, and then,
         the next time I push the button, a subtle but sweet
         perfume.

4

A grenade in my hand,
   but it turns out to be
      a large seed-pod
         which bursts
scattering its milkweed-like seeds
   which float away,
      but the law of gravity
         has been suspended

so the seed parachutes
   describe entirely unpredictable arcs
      to where they land
         and germinate.

OF INTEREST

Both of them bark,
    but one of the pair of dogs
fiercely guarding the house
    on the road to the woods

retreats, back
    to the barn
where the horses
    shudder and stamp.

The other one comes with me
    to the woods by the river,
the trillium woods.
    Millions of trilliums
preaching to me
    like stars.

He does not notice them,
    but he notices
the smells of the things
    of interest to him.

THE RIVERS OF GOD ARE FULL OF WATER

Today, I diverted water
    through a tiny channel
into a drying pond
    and felt a little like the kind of god
who alters the course
    of minor histories,
a tributary son of Scamander:

a few frogs leaped away
    from my approach;
a few fish and their shadows darted
    into the freshening pond
before I turned away.

Victor (Alzheimers) casts about
for the name of his condition
(because I inquired). "It's called
'Disasking'," he says distinctly,
relieved to have remembered,
at last.

VISITING POET

The poet is putting up a visiting
poet overnight, his wife none too pleased.
I've brought them a sleeping bag
but in the jumble in the back of the car
I only find the little blankets
from my granddaughter's crib.
I'll have to go back, but first
I remember I've bought the poets something,
a bottle of Crown Royal.
When I find it, the top has broken off;
it has crashed against
a bottle of scotch: a crazed shape
inside a fancy shopping bag.
We're remembering the broken glass
the last time this poet visited;
someone drank wine
from a glass with a crack in it.
My hands are covered with tiny splinters of glass
and I want to ask if I may wash them, please.
"What is the shape of this?" I ask. The poet host confides,
"Our friendship grew in the shadow
of my mother's death, which pulled on it like a moon."

LIQUOR CONTROL ON CUMBERLAND STREET

She pushes her guitar and backpack ahead of her in a
                                                shopping cart,
   her affable mutt attached to it by his leash.
We peer through the barred door to find out what time the
                                                store opens
   on a Sunday, and it's not til noon.
When I suppose we can last that long, she shows me her
                                                trembling hands:
   "I'm not so sure . . ." then "See you at noon,"
she calls out over her shoulder, and waves
   as we go our separate ways.

It's a phrase book, he's keeping his Italian up,
    keeping the tools sharp.
He wants to go back to Rome
    which feels like home, he says.
There's a girl there, more than a friend,
    she made plans to visit once,
though she couldn't afford the journey in the end,
    but it meant something that she wanted to come,
it must mean something, eh?
    maybe everything.
He's a welder, but it's hard to find a job
    at a distance with no connections, no family there.
He's talking to people here,
    and he's going back to look.
He'll get it together, hold it together
    at last, to last: *la saldatura.*

An SUV screeched
   and veered
     and braked
   and bolted forward
     and skidded into a ditch,
and the driver,
   a young woman,
     angry and frightened,
   fled from it
     into the field
       across the way
where a young man
   followed her
     and drunkenly argued
       and wrested the car keys
     out of her hand.
And I thought I might
   just stay in my yard
     and keep on raking leaves
but ran up and
   found them seated
     bucolically
side by side on the fringe
   of the meadow
     calling each other foul names.

When I asked her
   what she wanted
      me to do
he threatened me
   and swore,
but she grabbed
   the keys:
      "I just want to get him home."
We got him back
   into the car
      where he mumbled
      filth.
"I'll be in my yard if you need me,"
   I told her slowly
      and clearly so that
he'd understand.

She thanked me politely
   and drove away smoothly,
      carefully slow.

HARBOURED

we seek an explorer rose equal in weight
to our sorrows and able to stay with us to wait

we carelessly sink our hearts in the last days of June
wasting our time as we watch the moon inflate

only to see it fade in the second half
and desert its charge to divert us or placate

seeming to demonstrate how a foolish art
comes to relieve the heart, but to dissipate

genuine feeling then, at the very hour
tulips are closing, crickets begin to grate

harsh on the ears of the kids who believe in song
however arcane the words they cannot translate

sparrows in hymns and insects on summer nights
are never again to wonder about their fate

THE DETROIT INSTITUTE OF ART, AT NIGHT, AFTER THE ATTACKS OF 9/11

Gigantic stars and stripes
   snap manically against
      an arctic desert wind.
This neoclassical block
  of public architecture
     is the bridge of a ship of state
buffeted by gale-force blows
   and all hands stowed somewhere below,
     guarded or threatened
by a geometric black
   hulk called Gracehoper.
    And with these stripes
we are not necessarily healed.
   And there are stars
     beyond these stars.

POEM IN WHICH A GENTLEMAN IS WASHING HIS HANDS, IN A FAR ROOM

Two green bottles lie on their sides
on the sideboard, in them their wine
is aging imperceptibly, staining the corks;
the dyes in the printed draperies fade
in the always angled light of the sun;
dustmotes, breadcrumbs settle on the patterned weave
of carpet, the clouding furniture wax;
glues dry, finials dessicate, the tenons
of cross-pieces separate from the mortices
of chair- and table-legs;
a seat-cushion's fabric under the weight
of schoolbooks tears microscopically;
the breast feather of a flopping sparrow
flutters against the window-glass
and casts a minor shadow on the sheers;
a woman's scent disperses amidst the molecules
of warmed, accustomed air.

IL MARRONE MONDO

Now, all the edges are obscure;
   the details of our draperies
      dissolve in the mud.
If anything shines,
   it is only the paint
      we're painted in.
At the centre, some holy event
   casts light into the gloom
      but not very far.

Surely the master who put us here
   was wrong. In the photos
      of us from the moon
we are always bathed in light,
   in the bright gold and blue
      of the thirteenth century.

But our gestures, the poses
   chosen for us, are right,
      are not embarrassing or false,
   however unfamiliar
      in these later days.
A blessed joy should open the world
   not narrow it to certainty which is only
      another kind of blindness.

Attitudes and habits of prayer these days:
 "O shit," we say, "what do *I* know?"
  So, we're still praying then,
but the other direction,
  towards the murky edges of the painting,
   what navigators would call "dead reckoning."

The centre is always attentive,
 and calm. Light,
  let there be
  more such light.

TO GIVERNY

Voici inopinément un jeune garçon,
Coiffé de deux chignons en forme de nuages.
Il rit de me voir si tard chercher la voie de l'immortalité.

Li Bai, trans. Dominique Hoizey

That day, between the Gare St. Lazare
and Gare St. Lazare were
the natural wonders of Giverny:
a banquet of colours,
and at its core
the arc of a bridge
entwined with wisteria
where a Japanese boy and girl,
their brushes dipped in ink,
drew what they saw
so that we looked again
to see what they saw.
When we arrived,
the summer staff
were pruning the rose trees.
The willows leaned down
to the pond,
as we departed.

Waiting that morning
for our train to Vernon
we became aware
of a girl wearing a mask
or bandages;
we looked long enough to see
she was terribly disfigured,
the leper of St. Lazare,
or an accident.
The boy in the beautiful blue dress
may have been her
guardian angel,
though he did not notice her,
did not stare,
as we did, at the pair of them.

THE WORKERS

1 LES RABOTEURS DE PARQUET

At D'Orsay,
the Caillebotte workers
are scraping the floor
in a beautiful world
in which one works;
one kneels
but without the loss
of one's dignity.
It is possible sometimes
to talk and work.
The sheen on their skin
and the sheen on the painting
are the same.
The wood will be varnished
again, but for now
it is plain
and beautiful.

Elles portent des tabliers blancs, les blanchisseuses,
ses cheveux coiffés à la mode, en chignon;
elles plient les draps énormes, luisants, les repasseuses,
comme en chœur silencieux elles les secouent:
les voiles rectangulaires, les brassées de bannières,
ce corps de ballet dans cet atelier
élégant, voûté, au viaduc des arts,
comme des figurantes sur un écran.

Les draps luisent, comme les dos en sueur
des raboteurs sur la toile de Caillebotte;
on voit leur travaux comme une vue charmante:
c'est beau, c'est artificiel, c'est vrai.
Avec sa toile l'aube efface les étoiles.

3 I SPAZZINI

After the chipping away of marble
    in the Duomo floor
the grit left behind
    by its careful *restauratori,*

after the falling of chestnuts
    and leaves in the village square
through the air sweet with harvest
    no longer warm, not cool

after the passage of tourists
    beyond their crumbs, their trash,
when those who endure the endless
    mess of the place return

the sweepers come
   to work and to grumble
or swear: *È tanto, tanto,*
   ma non troppo, non.

4 THE PELLEGRINAIO OF SANTA MARIA DELLA SCALA, SIENA

The castaway infants of Siena,
see, some of them climb a ladder to Our Lady
blithely through the imagined vault
of Saint Sorore's mother's dream.
Sorore himself in his cobbler's tunic and cap
kneels to be given money by a bishop,
and so the story says the Ospedale
Santa Maria della Scala begins.

    The waiter in the piazza would not believe
    the story we told him of the gettatelli: no,
    the Sienese would never throw children away.

Our fate then to be trampled or to ascend on high:
one worker with bricks is almost under the hooves
of another bishop's roan who has ridden
theatrically to give alms to the hospital.
Other builders, like those infants, climb
to a scaffold above the imperilled man.

There is nothing scriptural in any of these scenes.
It is the work of the hospital that interests di Bartolo:
the wet-nurses and teachers in the daycare
stare where the children learn and play;
in the ward of the wounded and sick,
a portly friar hears a dying man's confession,
an attendant holds up a glass jar of urine.

The two naked men on these walls have nothing to do
with classical Greece; they are simply their needy selves:
one of them (posed like the man undressing himself
in della Francesca's *Baptism*) is dressing himself
in the clothes he has been given,
the other, anguished and grateful, is being bathed
before the great gash in his leg can be closed and dressed.

> *From Badesse's industrial park in the valley below*
> *an amplified voice so muffled it cannot be understood:*
> *is it announcing a strike? a delivery? an accident?*
> *an imminent danger? A voice in the wilderness.*

Della Francesca must have been Bartolo's apprentice,
he knew his master's workers well.
See how in the Arezzo scenes he notices the men
who sweat, the ones who lift the beams,
and the ones who wait, who hold the horses' reins.
For him there are no angels merely filling space,
no angels of any kind other than working angels,
the one who visits Mary, the one sent to Constantine.
There are no children of any kind, although
everything he paints depends on the baby as yet unborn.

At a table in the Badessa trattoria where his parents work,
their child is surrounded by waiters, kitchen staff,
customers and councillors,
who make a fuss and celebrate:
Bambino tra Santi e Patroni.
Ah, sí. Amen.

AGREEABLE NOISE

Some days a sonata
for violin and piano says

    reegy reegy skreeka
    tinkally clonk

and nothing more.

BEESONG

Humble bee
    how many blossoms
        stitched together
by your improvised
    predestined flight

        how many human minds?

THE NOISY ONES

The mist lifts off the lake;
  hidden along the edge
    the rustle of birds and small mammals.
A black duck splashes
  and lifts away from Black Duck Bay.
The clink of breakfast dishes
  from the houseboat
    tied to the other shore
is the first of human noises.

Soon there will sound screen doors,
  outboard motors, hammering down on the dock,
    trucks signalling reverse, air-brakes hissing,
and later, planes revving for take-off,
  jet-skis doing wheelies.

When we are thought of at all,
  we are thought of as some of "the noisy ones":
    the belligerent crows and anxious loons,
    busy woodpeckers, gathering geese,
    and us.

BIRD BRAINS

1 WOODPECKER

How many mornings
will you bash your head
against this metal pole
supposing that at last today this once
it will yield to your attack
some unmetal grub?

2 HUMMINGBIRD

How irresistibly sweet
must this beebalm be
for you to linger here
next to my hand,
ignoring me?

TWO GULLS, HIGH ABOVE, AT NOON

Silver pen-knives
   they fold, flash and vanish
at play, then pivot,
   bloom into spilt milk
under the cool gaze
   of a pale sliver of moon.

PIANISSIMO

What I'd like is everything
unpackaged, no more need
to fight through shrink-wrapped
cardboard and styrofoam
containers to get to the nourishment.
Or to peel away flakes
of tinfoil and waxed paper
just for the sake
of a little life-saver.

The noise, the endless noise, here
in the terminal, of edibles being released
from their packaging. The effort,
the struggle involved,

      even of getting dressed
and undressed, though buttons are quiet,
and zippers are almost inaudible.

THE BACH SUITE

For Zailig

PRELUDE (BACH IN TIME)

There's a moment after a fugue has begun
when it veers off the trail of the original key
into the woods, the wilderness: a mere accidental
deflecting you into the unpredictable and astonishing
    terrain
of potentially infinite modulations. You can stand the
    excitement
partly because you trust Bach to get you back on track.

There's another moment when you've finally cleared
    through enough underbrush
to see the trail again; you feel relief as the light breaks
    through. You can hear the ground.

In the middle there's a moment when it's as tangled as it's
    going to get,
the threads are knotted
and tugged. You pause; it's exciting, but you relax.
The rest of the journey is home.

ALLEMANDE (MY MOTHER AND BACH)

There's music I want you to hear, I say to her,
and then press Play. *O good*, she says,
as long as it isn't Bach. And it is,
or was going to be. *It's too restless,*
it sounds like a bunch of notes.

And it is. So I hesitate years later, when she wants to hear
my harpsichord, to play Bach for her. But she says,
Of course, play Bach. And she loves it, she says, and falls asleep.

Your mother is your point of departure,
the one you are always growing away from.
I'm listening to the 'cello suites, and wondering how
the same things can console you, calm you completely,
and at the same time open the range,
the almost limitless range, of being human,
unless they are Bach and your mother.

COURANTE (BACH LIMITED)

Infrequently, you can see
through Bach. You catch him
moving forward by means
of brilliant technique
and the will to proceed.
He does things because
he has to or because they fit.

Perhaps plough horses feel
that way when the earth
behind them yields too easily,
and the day is almost done.
Whether it's smug you feel
or ashamed, the moments of such
discovery are obscured
by the shock of disbelief.

SARABANDE (BACH AS JOB)

However auspicious the gales, however cruel,
however becalmed the ships, it's all weather.

However severe the dissonance, however long
the pauses, the silences, there's nothing but music.

GIGUE (ANIMATED BACH)

Another glass of wine might give you the courage,
even with guests peering over your shoulder,
to sit down at the harpsichord and play;

but another glass of wine and your fingers will lose
their memory of what's about to happen,
will wander and stumble like a comedian.

You've had moments of perfectly balanced inebriation
so that the fingering in an unfamiliar passage
was brilliant, was perfect, and unrecoverable;

but you're fairly certain this isn't one of those moments.
Sober up a little; try to be worthy.
Or better, play Handel. You're not too drunk to play Handel.

PRACTICAL ORDER ON ROAD 110 SOUTH NEAR STRATFORD

Officium, Jan Garbarek and the Hilliard Ensemble

Lines from Shakespeare leak into the dreams
of actors in their beds on Sunday morning.

East of the Festival, an infection may be contained
in the Sebbens' chicken barn: biosecurity is in effect,
kiddy-cars and a Shock Rocker Pool Float lie strewn on the
    lawn.

Early trucks travel the section's straight lines.
Cordwood piles by the woodlot and an abandoned truck
wait to be taken apart, restacked and burned.

Squeals and a man's yelling and whiffs of stink
drift across the field from the pig-barn on the next road
where they're loaded onto a livestock hauler one last time:
parce mihi with commentary and ornament.

A lavender tissue-flower blown from a bridal car
lies in the dust of the shoulder: *pulcherrima rosa.*

VARIANCE ON ROAD 110 NORTH
NEAR STRATFORD

Stravinsky, *Histoire du Soldat*

Crows add percussion to the *pasodoble*: caw caw caw;
a small flock of pigeons rises in widening circles
over the bean-field, making up their collective mind.

A couple of Canada geese join the gang ground-feeding
farther away; when they're adequately fed,
they lift into a kind of wedge and head south.

The rifle barrel flashes silver like a lance
at the side of the young man who walks ahead
of the van as it stops and starts on its way

through the dull grey-gold of stubble.
The occasional muffled thuk signals the likely end
of another groundhog's struggle to survive.

  Next day the ribbon between the wheel tracks
  will be stitched unevenly by the random
  touchings-down in the flight of a dozen cabbage whites.

PLENITUDE AND CONFORMITY,
IN THE LEASIDE LONGO'S

Striggio, *Ecce Beatam Lucem*

Flats of garden mums arranged in masses by colour
are banked along the edge of the parking lot

where suv's in compliant waves find sufficient room, and pause;
uniformed kids load oversized autumn planters into their
     cargo space.

Inside we negotiate the aisles in an orderly fashion
with ceremonial ease and confidence

past ranks of emerald bottles of mineral water,
boxes of pasta: fusilli, farfalle, pennoni,

and mounded polished apples of every available kind
to be divided among our individual baskets and carts.

Single voices secede from the smaller choirs.
A family tastes cheeses from around the world:

"It says to me, 'Why bother?' Not much bite."
We do not expect a revelatory peak

here on this plane of recurrent riches and choice;
we gel, we acknowledge each other,

we wait for the promised bakery bell.
We politely return our carts to their corrals.

SIDETRACKED, AT CHARNY

Berg, *Violin Concerto*

The startling undersides of poplar leaves
flicker in the early morning stormfront;
the streetlights suddenly go out.

At the tire centre, a sleepy guy
starts to rotate tires;
a crow lifts from the telephone wire
into the rising wind.

In the cerulean O's of aboveground pools
the filtered water
diluted with occasional raindrops
circulates.

This train is an anguished grieving:
everything's moving;
    we're not moving.

MINOR APOCALYPTICS AT HOME

Messiaen, *Quattuor pour la fin du temps*

The sun is not yet above the suburban houses,
the air remembers the chilly night it has come through;
it is a morning of soft fire and heavy dew.

The school buses flash a cautionary sign:
you must stop now, there is a maximum fine.

The filter pump has left a narrow fan
of sand on the driveway, and a wider one of wet.

It's garbage day *and* recycling day;
some of this stuff is going into the ground,
some may be redeemed.

The birds have agreed to one more round of rounds.
The last roses of summer are showing off,
without a trace of irony or sentiment;

there is more of heaven on earth than our practised cynics
and this bleary-eyed school boy will allow.

A NEW PSALM, OF ACCURATE PRAISE

To sing a new song,
    but not about myself:
the fragrance of flowers
    in fragrant unflowery words.

A friend admired the novels of George Eliot
    in a lecture yet felt obliged to indicate
        their characteristic imperfections.
He has written a couple of novels himself.
    Perhaps you have heard of them.

Sounds half-hearted,
    audenesque,
        though it needn't be.
"Oh, excellent nipples!"
    the obstetrics nurse told Leslie,
        "he'll have no trouble with these."

Equals science. An itemized list of creation with faithful
    diagrams
        and sufficient explanations.
Creator: "Thanks for paying attention, for caring enough
    to try to figure things out."

The beloved excels her poems /
   his poems, in everything but immortality,
      occasionally.

: a creek describes its bed,
   does not dry up, and
      does not flood its plain.
A creek attunes its bed.

   Spring-fed is praise.
      O hidden source!
         "O liquid dulcitude!"

A NEW PSALM, OF UNCERTAINTY

How shall we speak of you, O God?
   Is the thunder crack your angry voice?
      Are we children huddled under a blanket of faith?

We are needy, O God, and we need to tell you so.
   We need plants to grow, and come to grain or fruit.
      We need animals to offer their milk, and themselves.

We need a roof or tarpaulin, a blanket, a cup.
   How shall we speak to you, O God?
      If we beg, do you listen to us?

Hear us, O God, in our neediness and fear,
   And in our uncertainty, here,
      In our threadbare faith.

A NEW PSALM, OF VAULTING

God, you are here in the vigour of my limbs,
   in the flexibility of my back
      and the workings of my inner ear.

With you beside me, I pause
   to focus my mind
      and then I begin to run.

You balance me over the horse,
   you know which way is up
      when I tumble and twist.

You know where my feet and hands are,
   and the mat.

You keep my spotter alert
   to the angle and torque of my spine.

You are the sweetness
   of my fruit-flavoured sports drink;
      the attentiveness of the people in the stands.

When I nail the landing,
   you raise my arms.

You watch me rise and fall,
   and stand again.

Here I am, O God,
　　in this endless trench.
The walls of it rise up,
　　they rise up high above my sight.
I slog through the mud
　　my gear on my back.
My gear is a burden
　　it does not bring me relief.
I carry photos from home
　　the sight of them makes me weep.
If there is a sky above me
　　I fear it is full of bombs.
Where are you now, O God?
　　Are you at the end
Of this tunnel?
　　Are you in some possible sky?
Help me to see you
　　in this faceless mud.

A NEW PSALM, OF UNKNOWN IRONIES

The scrim, the barrage
   of misinformation,
      of half-truth and spin

erase for us individual sorrows, O God,
   erase accidental meanings,
      and touching coincidence.

Because we cannot afford them,
   and cannot bear them:
      the news erases a million tragedies.

It makes us wonder, O God,
   what we can
      afford, and what we can bear.

In self-defence I send jpg images
   of my granddaughter, to family and friends,
      as if there were no war.

A NEW PSALM, OF THE OBOIST

God's orchestra is encouraging,
　　the music blooms and mounts,
　　　　we are lifted up with it, we are improved.

The orchestra of God is capacious,
　　the harmonies are rich, complex,
　　　　the melodies soar, we're a little overwhelmed.

I am an oboist in the orchestra of God;
　　I colour the sound around me,
　　　　or disappear into the noise.

Occasionally I have a solo to play,
　　a minor cry from the heart before the strings
　　　　sweep in again and carry us away.

I do what I can, I play the notes
　　with all the feeling my skill allows.
　　　　We hope for the best; we try to watch your baton.

A NEW PSALM, OF STRANGENESS

Strange are your ways, O God:

You raise high the sequoias and giant redwood forests;
    You bring them to earth with a swipe of your muscled arm.

You haul us up out of the mud,
    And cause us to fall for no apparent reason.
You fill the oceans with little fishes,
    To feed them to bigger fish.

You fill the heavens with stars of every size and description;
    You situate us at the edge of one of the galaxies.

You rein in the horses of animosity,
    And unleash the dogs of storm.

You bury the tumour deep inside the brain;
    You train and guide the surgeon's hands.

You cause the microbes to increase in strength;
    They learn to resist the drugs you lead us to make.

Strange also, O God, are human ways:

We admire the earth from space stations we have
    constructed;
    We poison it manufacturing un-necessities.

We create anti-virals to control every new disease,
    And let the people of Africa die.

Strange are your ways, O God, and difficult,
    Strange also are the ways of us on earth.

HARD PLACE

Then through the bald, unfeathered air
and coldly, as a man would walk
against a metal backdrop, he
bore down on her

P.K. Page, "Only Child"

The baton hovers, then sticks. Not at a *fermata*.
Someone must have pressed pause to induce
this paralysis and not just in the conductor.
Some panic has persuaded the orchestra
there's nothing to be gained from detaching yourself
from the branch, nevertheless you prepare
for liftoff as if it were still an enviable fate.
You continue to await the expected downbeat,
you bravely resist the urge to give in to despair.
Then through the bald, unfeathered air

you suddenly stretch your limbs as if to descend
but instead you are rising through a liquid, thick,
towards the light and whatever air may be
miles above you. You have scales and fins
and a flexible strength, but, straitjacketed,
once again you fear the worst: endless headlock
no matter how much you squirm, resist, shake off
that hold to find room enough at last to dream,
instead of so purposefully merely taking stock,
and coldly, as a man would walk

into the frozen attitudes and uncertainties
of a hostile boardroom with a necessary plan.
How might he progress from this impasse?
By the heroic but minimal individual effort
to distinguish his own particular thoughts
from the haze and rush of opinions and ennui
that flash and blur in the unknown media
expanding and morphing apparently at will
around him, or more accurately as if free
against a metal backdrop, he

pulses like a cursor of flesh and blood
on this screen of unwritten and unforeseeable endings.
His curious narrative so far encouraged us that,
as if we knew what it might mean for him,
we prayed for a prosperous voyage, and he sailed
in the earth, *lentissimo*, through the aquifer,
his ship seeming to stall, had she way in her yet?
Whereupon all the terrestrial winds' hoarded,
directed intent (or indifference, if you prefer)
bore down on her.

HABEAS CORPUS

The body of the murdered man
    was wrapped
        and dropped from the back
          of a truck in a field
where I walk,
    but I did not happen to see
        that hopeless cocoon.

Some trees in that field
    by reason of their species
or being sheltered by a cedar bank
    have held onto their leaves
        and keys,
        their papery castanets,
until now: in the breeze
    a whispered polyphony
        of Christmas wishes,
          and fears.

A friend of mine once came
    upon a body tangled
      in a river bank
and what are the chances of that
    in this mostly peaceful place?

A kind of bell, a halyard,
   rings against its aluminum flagpole,
      but without a flag, no perfect leaf
   on a featureless field.

AN END OF READING

Mary,
   a Daycare Worker
      with toddlers in tow
on an outing
   to the nature preserve
      or the library,
is visiting Barnard
   at his desk
      in the wilderness.
Four very curious
   angioletti peek past her,
      and around her skirts.

She places her hand on the page of his writing:
   "Look at this," she may be saying,
      and pointing, "Think about this."
Or maybe she's saying "Stop.
   Stop reading, Barnard.
      Stop writing now."
Perhaps she means
   "These words refer to me. Look up,
      I am here."

From her own life she knows that moment
   when the book falls away,
     when the angel arrives to say,
"You are
   what you have been reading about.
     Arise."

CREDO

FACTOREM CÆLI

Most days don't need heaven; here's enough.
Don't even like the sound of it, what I've heard:
all those people, and me not good in crowds.

Why would anyone want to be immortal?
What would you do every day all day, if they call it
day there? And rest eternal sounds the same, but night.

When I dream of reaching to hold you, my arms go through
    you;
I hear your voice, but it comes from too great a distance;
you appear in a crazy story, then you vanish.

What I want heaven for, more than anything,
is to see you again. I need to see you again.
In heaven I want to hear you, and see you, and hold you.

Small twisting clouds like human
cannonballs fired from the other
side of the crest of the hill –
the mistral propels them
in an ephemeral arc.

A dark bird perched invisibly
in the olive tree waits out the wind
while three magpies, like schoolboys
up to no good, congregate,
disperse, swoop towards and away,
occupy the tree, abandon it.

They open the shutters to the sun
in the house above, then close them
against the wind;
the caught corner of this house roars.

EX PATRE NATUM

God is a god. The beard we recognize, comes
from patriarchy, not the other way round.
It is human to humanize gods; a man
with a falcon's head was a falcon first, divine.
Jesus is like Europa's bull one level up,
one level away from the earth, or the truth;
his seductive charms were considerable,
coming to us like one of us (but male).
That naked body on the cross is a disguise;
under that flesh and bone is a god, like a rock.

PROPTER NOSTRAM SALUTEM
(PREVENT US IN ALL OUR DOINGS)

Her toe points over the curb,
she waits for the walk sign,
her weight tips, she follows her foot
down to the street, crumpling
gracefully, a genuflection toy –
brakes gone, steering gone.
Her companion hooks her bent arm,
a nestling's wing, so that she does not
quite complete her fall, her fingers pitch
a glancing tent on the pavement.

EX MARIA VIRGINE

Dear lady of the subways, you whose heart
is a target-valentine of cupid art,
the non-pareil unparalleled you stand
co-equalized, competing with a land
of sunshine – "holiday in paradise" –
whose skinful glories make you look like ice;
a stonied pity in your gentile face,
you, picture of a sculpture, in your place
across the tracks, is it even dirty there?
Do boys with crayons blasphemously swear?
O paper rose of the junkpile, lost to day,
O cardboard virgin of the M.T.A.,
with white and black decayed to shades of gray,
teach us to pray, teach us a better way.

CRUCIFIXUS ETIAM

In the subway train, scrubbed
boys and girls are barely contained
by their school uniforms;
old women are shrouded to the neck
in shawls they think they need;
and a lady with crooked legs
tries to straighten her seams.
Once in a topless bar in New York
Marshall McLuhan was heard
to remark, "no, they ah wear
nakedness," and that is why

their nakedness is nothing.
Porno movies, clothing stores conspire
to make us look the same, not beautiful.
If we could bear to let ourselves
be seen, He might then say to us
Today, in paradise.

"Geese, are you of this world
or the spirit world?"
"We are flying south, and
we are flying home."
"Great Cedar, are you a spirit tree?"
"I have been green all winter.
Warm days I shall shed my balm around.
Today I hold my scent within me
until I am bruised. Bruise me."

The resurrection body is clearly not like this one:
    your friends and family don't know you,
    they never know where you'll show up next.
In the nest of last year's leaves along the drive
    I search for gravel eggs, to throw them back.
    And all those fish, those straining nets,
    they couldn't eat everything they caught.
The congregational responses are the rumbling
    thunder of a thin, adulterated joy.
A boy whacks his head with a little book,
    blows raspberries, makes smacking kissing sounds,
    which pretty much covers it.
A big man in vestments shouting, babies howling.
    Where is the choir? They are not here;
    they have risen, apparently.
Eggs on the altar, for the children to find,
    like hunters in camouflage
    and neon vests. When exactly is time full?

1

Sunburnt roofers don't have much time
for the view:
other people's neighbours' yards.

2

"Slime had they for mortar"
and they builded high,
too high.

3

The king is dead.
The castle is sand, or becoming sand;
the king is dead.

4

"See the seagull on the statue's head?
He thinks he's king.
And the one on the arm who wants to be."

5

"Brug is mine, Mortimer,"
said Henry,
"Wigmore too."

6

Perched on the highest branch of that tree,
you cannot see
into the tree.

CUM GLORIA

1

Not his curly hair, his cotton overalls
narrow the cashier's eyes as he flies
to the counter giving his coin to her
and vanishing,
    but his earring of shining gold.

2

Last night the petioles of leaves
outside these windows froze;
now the house is full of light
as it is, not screened, not stained
the customary green
    the ephemeral gold.

CUIUS REGNI

You can't get there on holiday
in a rented car, I said;
the kingdom is not accessible
to tourists.
At Christmas in Lahaina once
I went to a church that had no walls,
no visible walls.

But You, mulatto Lord,
in a Caribbean holy land
in the church of St. Martin of Tours
in Marigot, on New Year's Day,
rebuked me, saying:
The kingdom is where
you are, it is
always accessible.

However soft the showers of rain
the honey-milky, buttery light,
however warm the turquoise sea,
Your will be done.

How little here I understand,
how little it matters what I do,
how little it depends on me,
Your will be done.

I find it harder to discern
Your will in such a foreign place;
foreign to me but not to You;
Your will be done

IN SPIRITUM SANCTUM

It seemed to me
   I had dreamed a dream
      so consoling

        (of a family seated
        in a bright meadow,
        or on the fresh linens
        of a wide bed)

that the burden
   of living
      was eased.

QUI CUM PATRE ET FILIO (NOT GRINDING)

Poised at a slight tilt on the island slope
beside the pile of graying logs
sprouting at both ends bent spikes
the boy still in his polo pyjama bottoms
with one hand pours from a dinted turpentine tin
lake water spurting in glugs into
the rusted can nailed to the rickety brace
which pees a steady arc onto the grindstone
as with his other hand he cranks
the ponderous disk,
and his father, sweat on forehead, angles
the axehead, shoves it sizzling against
the smooth rough spinning round
while it sprays long drops, fine stone chips.

The handle fixed to the axle loose
in the stone, slips and jerks, then turns
with the wheel as the boy lets it spin,
hypnotized by the dazzle below where
the lake surface crinkles in the breeze.

UNUM BAPTISMA

The water lapped like Latin
against granitic and schistose rock;
the lake lacked desecrating whining,
mechanical blasphemies,
was silently full
of only its own sounds.

The water, you said, was empty,
tasted of nothing,
as you passed the white cup to Christie
for her to drink;
even though by then you had bled into it
from your rock-cut knee some time,
after you slid on the living slime.
So, even though it seemed pure,
the water was a kind
of holy water.

IN REMISSIONEM PECCATORUM
(DIVINE APATHY, FLIGHT 490)

Woodlots and ploughed fields,
  riverbeds and roads,
and minuscule shining rectangles
  of human consciousness.
You might say "privacy"
  except that from this height
everything they do is knowable, and known.

A careless mortal desecrates the rite
  in a civic park;
he is morally ugly, but you are feeling
  benign, and let it pass.
In any case, his retribution is likely to come
  from someone closer to home,
and might just as well be banal.

Special offer, one day only:
  you let everything pass.
Or more properly you leave them
  to themselves;
but that means no visions either, no glimpses
  of flashing eyes, or shining hair.
All right, then, they're on their own.

Coming upon it unexpectedly
   Dialysis
   in the new hospital:
corridors, elevators, wings,
   everything rational
     and surprising, the opposite
     of luck; internal
rhymes, you suppose they may have been
at the ends of lines in earlier versions
   and been moved;
you're pleased to find them, not that you were
   looking, touched
   that they survived, a patient
working out, a thinking through without fretting,
   a patient in dialysis
who will be too old for surgery
   given the waiting list
who has pondered the Great Expected
   longer, more steadily than his friends
   being Irish to be blunt, say what you like.
Whither (but who says "whither" any more)
   never in doubt,
but as in a walk around a little lake
   the other shore is always familiar,
   and fresh:
marina, playground, lock.

POPE INNOCENT'S HOLIDAY IN SUBIACO, AUGUST 1202

The racket of cicadas and crickets,
  of farmers' carts and cooks,
  the apothecary's mortar,
and papal chaplains
  splashing below
  in one of Nero's lakes.

The greenness of the countryside
  reflects in the lake
  and makes of it a meadow;
in the decorated considerable tent
  pitched for the business of the Curia:
  scenes of nature in the midst of nature.

And Innocent himself gargles
  with refreshing water from the natural
  basins he finds on his walks.
How we are occupied, and how we are relieved:
  the apothecary lifts his jars
  of urine, into the morning sun.

BORN WRONG IN HOLY WEEK

For Gabriel

Cet homme défiguré, the old priest complained
in his homily, and indicated the crucifix;
disfigured too by faith and scholarship,
by history, sin and art, and by our needfulness.
But he survives his disfigurements.

You arrive, misshapen in the womb;
you face the terrified love
of your parents, and the rest of us;
malformé, you have changed everything
merely by being born.
   "Come in, come in, we were not expecting you,"
   shout the crowds at the gates of Jerusalem.
Conceived, received in love, you pull
love into shapes we did not know.

   The news: four American civilian infidels
   in Iraq, shot, burned, dismembered and hanged.
   Et ces deux frères, enfants battus,
   their Texas mother told by God
   to bash their skulls in with a rock, obeyed.
   Why be shocked?
   Why try not to be shocked?

But you, you have done nothing but live.
How you may live, or die, we do not know.
We want, *mon tout petit*, to be worthy of you.

END

when will the treadmill of life and death stop
each rebirth gets more confusing
until we discover the jewel of our mind
we're like blind mules following our feet
            The Collected Songs of Cold Mountain, 185, trans. Red Pine

The endlessness preys on my mind.
It's not a question of finding your feet.
Not only have we lost the ability to stop,
each rebirth gets more confusing.

The wartime roadsigns were deliberately confusing,
to deflect the invaders from places they had in mind.
You wonder when you hear a thousand feet
when will the treadmill of life and death stop.

Curious to increase the sound you pull out a stop
to fill the music with fractions. It's confusing.
We're lost once again in the swell of the mind;
we're like blind mules following our feet.

We slog through this poem of uneven feet.
Tired of its slide of stuff, we want it to stop
but wade through the slag which is only confusing
until we discover the jewel of our mind.

SHRINE

Even if there's a demonstrable there there
and you make appropriate arrangements for some peace
of mind, proportional to your allotted years,
nobody knows the place.

I know the face, but am quite unable to place
your outdated military accoutrements: you there,
me here, both of us still pursuing peace
after a hundred years.

You mind your ps and qs for years,
everything paid for and in its place
but now in what amounts to an untraceable there
motionless as peace.

And piecemeal he called this meagre quizzical peace.
You try calmly to reconstruct through the dismembered
    years
in the simulacrum of some touristy holy place
agony that enacted there.

CAGED

The cricket who
kept me company three days
has fallen silent,
I don't know where.

Jane Hirshfield, "Unnameable Heart"

Recalling my time in a cage before those days
of nattering backgrounds and muzak when silent
seemed blessed, I wonder where
the cricket who

befriended me, who
played in his own cage for days
and sang about what it means to be silent
is. I don't know where

to turn now, seem not to know even where
I am, and lament the one who
again on this day of all days
has fallen silent

as if being silent
were a necessary joke in these sites where
cages feel like caves and I remember who
kept me company three days.

MESSE

The outmoded theological clanking continues:
we observe the prospect, unaccountably cheerful
as some religious contraption fulfils its mission as dredge
and brings up a dripping jawful of marl.

What's the best we can do with this slough of marl?
The effort to find a semi-precious lining in our failures
    continues
and makes restorative gardeners more or less cheerful.
Click. Click. Goes the dredge:

the mess of confession, whatever it is we dredge
up in the anticipatory gleam of burning marl;
and yet the unlawful and demoralizing behaviour continues,
awful but cheerful.

They spar, they reconcile, they aspire to be cheerful;
with flour and assorted herbs and spices they dredge
fish fillets for dinner, one of the fish that escaped becoming
    marl.
All the untidy activity continues.

STAY

the capacity for
postponement – we shall put that
off the majesty of the mind
said, in the newspapers, walking among the blessed

                                      Jorie Graham, "Belief System"

Never mind
the circumstances, we shall ask for blessed
relief, a stay of execution, for
postponement – we shall put that

to the presiding magistrate so that
whatever comes to mind
in the interim will seem blessed:
the capacity for

consoling or deluding ourselves, for
exacting sufficient compensations, at least enough that
whatever the feverish mind
said, in the newspapers, walking among the blessed

convinces us he did feel a little blessed
by the distraction such as it was, for
the time being, unwilling to slice at least that
off the majesty of the mind

NOSTALGIA

Some mornings, tranquillized
by the shower's warmth
you don't want to be born
into the colder, drier bathroom air,
but eventually you pull the curtain back
on the rest of the day.
There's a faint image of you
in the misted mirror:
you'll get used to it, and the atmosphere.

You remember the pleasure of being bathed
    as a child by your mother,
    the warmth of the water, sweet smell of the soap
    the strength of her hand under your head
    as she tipped you backwards and rinsed your hair
    and gazed down into your eyes.
Now you imagine bathing everyone else in turn.
They relax in the warmth;
    the light in the bathroom is soft on their skin.
You soap their necks, their shoulders, their upper arms
    and rinse with your hands their necks, their shoulders,
                    their upper arms.
Everyone. And you may begin with anyone, and continue in
                      any order you like.
    A famous person. We live in an age of celebrity.
    Someone from work. From the neighbourhood.
    We live in communities. A relative. We have families.
    The boy behind the counter at the convenience store.
    The woman in the alto section of the choir.
    The man who walks his Lab on the Base Line
    early every morning. A woman with rosy cheeks
    by Gainsborough. A poet from the nineteenth century.

You gently soap his underarms, his breast,
    his sides, and belly. Her belly, her groin.
    Her secret crevices. His crevices, his protuberances,
    his thighs. Her knees, her ankles, her feet.
    Now rinse, cupping warm water over every curve,
    and plane, to lave each limb. Now playfully splash.
Begin again. This time, the movie star is a little child:
    her neck, her chest, her tummy, her little bum.
    Is an elderly man: his arms, his sagging breasts.
    His skin is dark as mahogany, and papery. This time
    her skin is olive and smooth, the graceful curve
    of a scar from her shoulder-blade down to her waist.
Now rinse her back, his legs, her hair. Soon you will lift
    him into a soft warm towel, and rub her dry.
Whatever happens is private; whatever happens,
    he will be clean at last, will have felt your loving hands.
Begin again. My body is soiled, and smells
until you wash away the dirt of the earth and myself.

ANNA'S LOVERS

Tolstoy's readers, we intuit each other
in our separate beds and chairs.
Vronsky kisses the palm of his hand
where Anna has touched it in farewell
as we fall asleep
our homemade and store-bought bookmarks
fall from our hands

and for one of us a flash
drive memory
stick in the form of a flexible wristband
eases with pressure into itself,
circling nothing.

We wait for him to win her over;
we attend on her.
In the earliest shadows of her doom
our radios on snooze will play
the Snow Maiden melodrama
all the way to the end,
or until their time runs out.

We dream in our various beds
hard and soft, narrow and wide.
Vronsky in his sleep touches
himself with his kissed hand.
Our houses glow both from within
and on the outside: their night lights
and an almost perfect
and wintry moon.

CEDARSMELL: AL PURDY

I'm digging a dead cedar out of the garden, Al,
when Avril comes outside to tell me she's just heard
someone on the CBC reading a poem she didn't know
by "the late Al Purdy." Easter weekend; we didn't know.
It's an evergreen, but it's dead, and the metaphor
is too hard to miss, and I wonder now
how many people had Purdyesque moments
while they heard the news. I could stretch this out:
the roots were tangled and tough to remove,
and the trunk was as fragrant as biblical Lebanon
when I sawed it in pieces. The smell sent me back
to a storage room in the basement of the house
I grew up in; we'd had it built after we came through a fire,
and lined it with cedar. It's not exactly the same
as the smell of cedargreen, but it guards things from moths,
and time. "If the firstfruit is holy, then so is the lump.
If the root is holy, the branches will be."
I saw what I sawed. This is getting embarrassing.
We'll be reading you forever, evergreen Al,
we'll be seeing the world forever, through your eyes.

FURNITURE

For Gordon Roper

You don't know by sight
    or weight the nearness
    of the end of the book,
so I give you the big
    biography of Herman Melville
    to hold before I begin to read
it aloud to you.

We listen together to the prose,
    the documents, the views,
but you know already much of what we hear;
how richly your mind is furnished
and you arrest the narrative
    periodically with a commentary:
    Redburn, houses you visited
    in New York, Hershel Parker himself.

The Parker biography begins with Herman
    as a boy in the company
    of his father as he slides into
    genteel poverty, the day he transports
    their furniture by barge to Albany.
"A home is created by furniture," you say
    in this pleasant room furnished out
    of your memory and your past
    with things you feel to know.

SWEET ONE HUNDREDS

My aunt tells herself to remain calm,
   vulnerable to panic as she knows she is.
It was only a documentary film
   on the dangers of nuclear war.
The light that shone from the strange cloud
   was nothing like this morning light.
The only genetic mutations she knows
   are those of her backyard tomato plants.
Nevertheless, a vague unease persists all week,
   a solemn sorrow she cannot measure or shake.

YOUR HANDS, YOUR EYES

For Joanna

Your hands worked carefully on and on,
carefully at every moment
on and on as you crocheted a tablecloth.
You had broken your ankle
out dancing, and had to be still,
stay in, but could not ever be idle.
You hooked the beige thread
into ornate, floral rings;
you attached those rings,
and a tablecloth
slowly filled your lap.
You were making use,
good use of your time;
you were making something
beautiful.

How thoughtfully you watched your hands
and each stitch in the thread.
Your hands and your friends' hands
made perogies in the kitchen
at Saint Casimir's,
countless perogies week after week,
along with endless laughter,
stories, and prayers, and talk.

And so years later I learned to crochet;
I haven't made a tablecloth
or anything so fine and elaborate.
I do not have your patience or skill,
or a broken ankle,
come to think of it.

I remember you clapping
and clasping your hands
together in delight.
I remember you
holding my face in your hands,
those hands, to look at me.

Gordie showed me how to hold a bird
   So that it wouldn't hurt itself.
Gave me headstarts in races
   Without making me think they were headstarts.
Played the right hand while I played the left
   When we had to practise the piano.
Took me to a horror movie,
   Told me not to be afraid.
Slid the silver of his father's sword
   From its leather scabbard.
Named the creatures with me,
   Right, like Adam, every time.
Pricked my finger for me, and his own,
   When we wanted blood for our microscopes.
Put a bullet through his brain
   Because he wasn't doing well enough at school.

THE SHAPE OF DUST

Burlap and blue plastic tarpaulins
in the shapes of what we love enough
to care for and wrap:
treelings, woodpiles, powerboats

Wrapped against the grit, the granular salt,
the crap the drains beneath car washes
fill with (something cleaned means
something else gets dirty somewhere else)

Sweet cigarette smoke
giving up the shape of those lungs,
a momentary smudge
in the shared air
before your own lungs reshape
the perfumed carbon

Airborne particulates sink into wetlands,
    (muck thou art).
Saharan dunes are blown across the Atlantic;
specks of the granular ghosts could land in sandtraps,
in bunkers to be whacked with expert wedges

But where does
        dust   rest?

FINALLY THE END OF POETRY

Finally,
  the end
    of poetry.
No more
  poems, or
    the need for them.
We shall write to each
  other now
    from the heart
with the best
  words we
    can find
in the full light
  of everything we know.

NOTES AND ACKNOWLEDGMENTS

In "The Rivers of God are Full of Water," Scamander is the river god who fought on the side of the Trojans (*Iliad*, XX and XXI).

The "explorer rose" in the ghazal "Harboured" refers to a variety of roses developed to survive Canadian winters.

Gracehoper in "The Detroit Institute" is the Tony Smith sculpture (1972).

The title of "Poem in Which a Gentleman is Washing His Hands, in a Far Room" refers to one of the lost paintings by Jan Vermeer.

The painting in "An End of Reading" is the *Apparition of The Virgin to Saint Bernard* (1486) by Filippino Lippi, in the Badia Fiorentina.

One of the kings in "Kings of the Castles" is Henry II of England.

The account of "Pope Innocent's Holiday in Subiaco" is based on a letter found by Karl Hampe, described by Helene Tillman in *Papst Innocenz III.*

"End," "Shrine," "Caged," "Messe," and "Stay" are glostinas, a form invented by Gabe Foreman and Josh Trotter that combines the glosa and the sestina.

"With One of a Set of Duelling Pistols" was published as "Gordie (I)" in *Moving to the Clear* (1976), ed. Dennis Lee. "Born Wrong, Holy Week" was first published in *What Surprises You* (2005).

Thanks to the editors of *Waves* where "Crucifixus etiam" was published as "Contemplation: Crucifixion," and the editor of the *Peterborough Examiner* who first printed "Cedarsmell: Al Purdy."

Thanks to Allan Hepburn and the others with the MacLennan Poetry Series for their candour, and for their rigorous and illuminating readings of the poems. Thanks to the little fish for their encouragement and friendship.

PERMISSIONS

Excerpt from Li Bai, "En Me Promenant sur le Mont Tai" translated by Dominique Hoizey, from *Li Bai : Sur Notre Terre Exilé*. Copyright © 1990 E.L.A. / La Différence. Reprinted by permission of La Différence.

Excerpt from "Only Child" from *The Hidden Room: Collected Poems* (Volume One) by P.K. Page. Copyright © P.K. Page, 1997. Reprinted by permission of The Porcupine's Quill and the Estate of P.K. Page.

Han Shan, #185, translated by Red Pine, from *The Collected Songs of Cold Mountain, Revised and Expanded*. Copyright © 2000 by Bill Porter. Reprinted with the permission of The Permissions Company, Inc., on behalf of Copper Canyon Press.

Except from "Unnameable Heart" from *The Lives of the Heart* by Jane Hirshfield. Copyright © 1997 by Jane Hirshfield. Reprinted by permission of HarperCollins Publishers and Michael Katz.

Excerpt from "The Bight" from *The Complete Poems 1927–1979* by Elizabeth Bishop. Copyright © 1979, 1983 by Alice Helen Methfessel. Reprinted by permission of Farrar, Straus and Giroux, LLC.